Sports Medicine

Sports Medicine

Scientists at Work
Melvin Berger

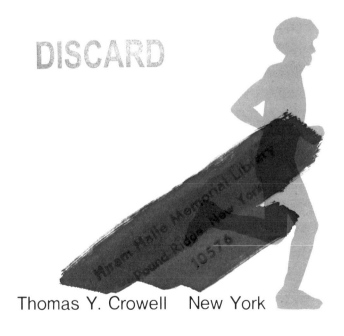

Thomas Y. Crowell   New York

45408

Library of Congress Cataloging in Publication Data
Berger, Melvin.
Sports medicine.
Bibliography: p.
Includes index.
Summary: Discusses the field of medicine
which attempts to treat and prevent sports-
related injuries.
1. Sports medicine–Juvenile literature.
[1. Sports medicine] I. Title.
RC1210.B37   1982   617'.1027   81-43891
ISBN 0-690-04209-4   AACR2
ISBN 0-690-04210-8 (lib. bdg.)

10 9 8 7 6 5 4 3 2 1

CONTENTS

1
What Is
Sports Medicine?

A famous football star is afraid his career is over because of a bad knee.

A player on a high school soccer team sprains his shoulder during a game.

A champion ice skater wants a training program that will get her into top shape for the day of her Olympic race.

A running-shoe manufacturer is trying to design the best possible shoe for joggers who run on hard pavement.

A pole-vaulter gets nervous at important meets, and never does as well as at practice.

A first-grader breaks her arm in a spill while roller skating.

A sixty-two-year-old man who has had heart surgery

wants to know whether it is safe for him to play tennis.

These individuals are typical of the many persons who need treatment, help or advice related to sports activities. In the past, such people would go to their doctor or coach, and get the standard medical or athletic attention. Now, more and more of them are turning to experts in the new field of sports medicine.

Simply put, sports medicine is the science of preventing and treating sports injuries. But it is more than that. It also includes building physical fitness, improving athletic skills, developing good mental health, and doing basic research on people and sports and sports equipment.

What muscles are used in a karate chop? These sports scientists are finding out.

(DR. PETER R. CAVANAGH, BIOMECHANICS LABORATORY, PENNSYLVANIA STATE UNIVERSITY)

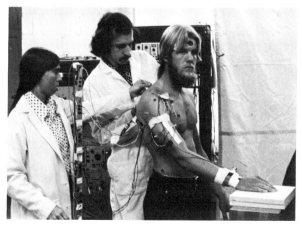

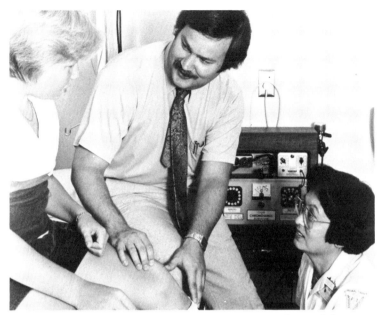

Orthopedic surgeons, such as Dr. Lewis Yocum, usually head the sports medicine team. Here he examines a young patient with the help of Registered Physical Therapist Grace Fukuto.
(NATIONAL ATHLETIC HEALTH INSTITUTE, CENTINELA HOSPITAL MEDICAL CENTER)

Who Are the Sports Scientists?

A number of different types of scientists are at work in the field of sports medicine. At the head of most sports medicine teams is the *orthopedic surgeon*. He or she is a medical doctor who specializes in treating diseases or deformities of the body's structure, including the bones, joints and muscles.

Orthopedic surgeons who work in sports medicine care for everyone—from the youngster with a pain in his knee to the star athlete whose career is endangered by a serious injury. The doctors treat their patients in various ways. They may suggest a few days of rest or give some special exercises. They may prescribe drugs, braces or casts. Or, in extreme cases, they may decide to operate.

Sports medicine doctors treat everyone from youngsters to star athletes, such as Magic Johnson of the Los Angeles Lakers, who is shown recovering from knee surgery. (CENTINELA HOSPITAL MEDICAL CENTER)

Working with the orthopedic surgeons are experts who study human structure and anatomy, and the effects of exercise on the body. They are called *certified athletic trainers, licensed physical therapists,* or *exercise physiologists,* depending on their particular training and background.

These specialists perform various jobs in sports medicine. They test the strength of the different muscles of the body. They measure the patient's lung capacity. By weighing the patient while submerged in a large tub of water, they learn the proportion of fat to lean tissue in his body.

Often the sports scientists develop special exercises for their patients. Mostly they design exercises to build up weak muscles. They also choose exercises that speed recovery after an injury, improve a person's skill or strength for a particular sport, or serve as part of a general fitness program.

Physical condition is not the only factor in sports success. Mental condition, which includes thoughts, feelings, fears, desire to succeed, and so on, is also vital. The scientists who study the relationships between mind and body are *psychologists.* Most psychologists hold advanced college degrees that qualify them to treat patients. The psychologists help athletes overcome any mental blocks that

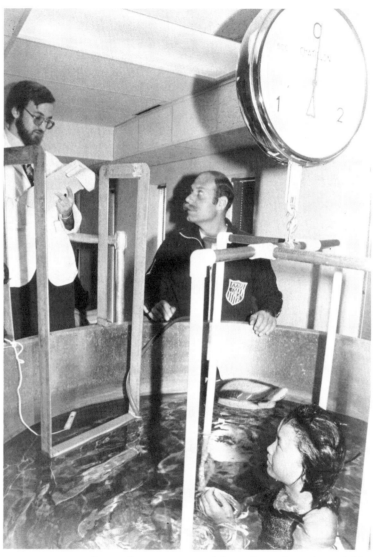

Sports scientists learn the proportion of fat to lean tissue by weighing the person in a giant tub of water.

(NATIONAL ATHLETIC HEALTH INSTITUTE, CENTINELA HOSPITAL MEDICAL CENTER;

PHOTO BY TONY PALEY)

may be interfering with their success in sports. By discussing their problems with them, the psychologists are often able to help athletes improve their performance, enjoy their participation, and generally become happier people.

Behind the scenes in sports medicine are many scientists at work in basic research. One important area of investigation is called biomechanics, the study of the human body as a machine. The experiments range from analyzing the motions of pitching, to learning which part of the foot strikes the ground first in running; from studying slow-motion movies of a tennis stroke, to applying the laws of physics to help a shot-putter throw farther. Most of the scientists doing work in biomechanics have advanced college degrees in biomechanics, medicine or a related field.

Other medical specialists are sometimes called in to help the sports scientists. Among them are the *podiatrists,* who are experts in diagnosing and treating conditions of the feet. There are also *cardiologists* (heart experts), *ophthamologists* (eye experts), *radiologists* (X-ray specialists), *dermatologists* (skin experts), *pediatricians* (experts on children's problems) and *internists* (internal medicine specialists). In addition, the sports scientist may consult with *nutritionists,* who help plan diets for athletes.

Sports scientists come from different backgrounds and

The study of the human body as a machine is called biomechanics. A researcher is getting ready to make high-speed films of the leg movements of a cyclist.

(DR. PETER R. CAVANAGH, BIOMECHANICS LABORATORY, PENNSYLVANIA STATE UNIVERSITY)

do a great variety of tasks. They hold many points of view. But in one way they are all the same. All care deeply about sports, and believe that athletics are a vital part of life.

Most men and women in sports medicine are, or were, active in sports themselves. They know how a college football player feels when he learns that he cannot play for the rest of the season. They know that many swimmers would do anything rather than miss a day of practice. And they know what distance runners mean when they say they "hit the wall."

Sports scientists understand the joys and satisfactions, the benefits and values, as well as the risks and dangers, of sports play. In their clinics and labs, their hospitals and offices, they are working to bring the delights of safe, health-giving sports to everyone.

Where Did It Start?

The idea that athletes need special care goes all the way back to ancient Greece. In those days the sports medicine doctors were called *gymnasts,* a Greek word that originally referred to those who trained and treated athletes. Hippocrates (460–377 B.C.), the father of modern medicine, was a gymnast for some of the early Olympic games held at Olympia in Greece.

Over the following centuries, though, sports medicine dropped in importance. Disease, plagues and starvation were killing whole populations. Doctors were extremely limited in the drugs and treatments that were available. They were mostly concerned with the survival of their patients. And since sports was such a small part of daily life, they saw little need to develop this branch of medicine.

The situation stayed about the same until early in the twentieth century. By then, medical science had advanced to the point where doctors could look beyond just prolonging life. Some began to think about improving the quality of life through physical fitness.

Three pioneer sports scientists, Robert Osgood, P. D. Wilson, and Gus Thorndike, established the first fitness laboratory at Harvard University in 1919. The lab was only concerned with the general study of fitness and did not treat sports injuries. Still it is considered the earliest sports medicine facility in the United States.

The first sports medicine centers, concerned with injuries as well as fitness, began opening in the mid-1950s. Since then the growth has been amazing. By 1980 about eighty-five sports medicine centers were in full bloom around the country. And new ones are opening all the time.

Why the Growth in Sports Medicine?

The rapid gain in sports science seems to have two basic explanations. First, the boom in sports participation. More leisure time, greater affluence, and increased availability of sports equipment and facilities are making it easier for people of all ages to take part.

It is estimated that about 55 million adults exercise daily, and that some 25 million youngsters under the age of 16 play at some sport after school.

Advances in modern medical science have made possible the growth in sports medicine. A sports scientist is getting ready to test physical fitness.

(NATIONAL ATHLETIC HEALTH INSTITUTE, CENTINELA HOSPITAL MEDICAL CENTER)

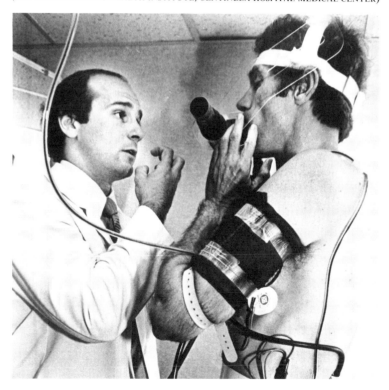

SPORTS MEDICINE

All this sports activity is surely improving the health and well-being of the players. But it is also increasing the number of sports-related injuries. An estimated 20 million adults and 10 million youngsters enter doctors' offices, sports medicine clinics, or hospital emergency rooms with sports injuries every year.

The growth of sports medicine is also due to the remarkable advances of modern medical science. Only recently has it become possible to prevent and treat successfully the many different kinds of sports injuries. But often it takes someone with a particular knowledge of sports medicine to treat these patients. Most traditional physicians are best at treating one part of the body— the heart, the eyes, or the kidneys, for example. What the hurt athlete needs are health professionals with expertise in treating one part of the population—those in sports and athletics.

Sports scientists fully understand sports injuries. They can advise athletes on how to prevent future injuries and help them to get back into play as quickly as possible. Further, they can offer suggestions on what to eat, what to wear, and how to improve the athlete's condition and game. And they can give answers to some difficult sports questions that only someone with a background in both athletics and medicine can provide.

2
A Sports
Medicine Center

It is about noon. Dr. Joseph S. Torg, Director of the University of Pennsylvania Sports Medicine Center, arrives at the Center. He is an orthopedic surgeon, and has just finished an operation at the nearby University Hospital.

Before seeing any patients at the Sports Medicine Center, Dr. Torg leafs through the charts of those who have afternoon appointments. They range from an injured high school football player to a girl recovering from knee surgery, from a professional soccer player who had hurt his leg to a college student after an ice-skating accident.

About 20,000 patients with sports-related injuries enter the University of Pennsylvania Sports Medicine Center every year. All pass under the brightly colored college banners to enter the Center. The large main room is light and cheerful. Near the entrance one finds the receptionist and chairs for the waiting patients. Behind are the exercise machines and the treatment tables. Still farther back is the area for making casts. Along one side are doors leading to the examining rooms.

Patient by Patient

Tom sprained his shoulder in a high school football game. He came to the Center after the game, and Dr. Torg fit him with a special sling. Now Tom wants to know if his shoulder is healed, and whether he can play in next Saturday's game.

Dr. Torg checks Tom's shoulder in one of the small examining rooms. Carefully he feels around the bones of the shoulder with his experienced fingers. He gently moves Tom's arm this way and that, asking Tom to tell him when it hurts. Then he studies the X-ray pictures.

The doctor tells Tom that his shoulder is still not healed. His arm will have to remain in the sling for at least another week. And he will not be able to play football for two or three weeks. Playing before the sprain is fully mended, the doctor says, might cause permanent damage. Expecting Tom's disappointment, Dr. Torg is ready with

A SPORTS MEDICINE CENTER

a program of exercises that will keep him in shape while his shoulder is recovering.

Twenty-two-year-old Kathy slipped while skiing, and slammed her left knee into a tree on the side of the slope. Dr. Torg had decided that an operation was necessary to repair the damage. Now it is two months after surgery, and Kathy is in for a checkup.

Certified athletic trainer Joseph Vegso places an elastic bandage on Kathy's knee.
(DR. JOSEPH S. TORG, SPORTS MEDICINE CENTER, UNIVERSITY OF PENNSYLVANIA)

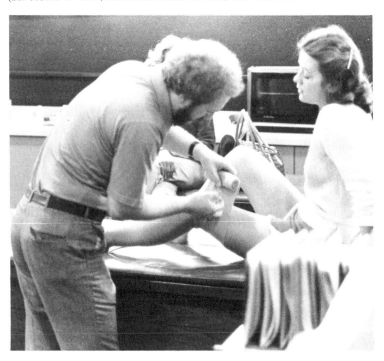

Joseph Vegso is helping Kathy onto a treatment table. He is one of the certified athletic trainers at the Center. Joe can tell by the way Kathy moves her leg that the knee is healing well. Her excellent progress shows that she is ready to move on to a new, more difficult set of exercises. Kathy promises to do them regularly at home. She knows that her recovery depends on how well she sticks to the schedule Joe is preparing for her. Finally, the trainer slips an elastic bandage around Kathy's knee, and explains when she should wear it.

Mary runs on her junior high school track team. For some months, though, she has been getting pains in her legs each time she races.

The podiatrist on the staff of the Sports Medicine Center, Dr. Gary Gordon, questions Mary about the exact kinds of pain she feels in her legs. He then asks her to walk back and forth across the room while he watches closely. After observing her leg and foot movements, Dr. Gordon asks her to sit on the table while he measures the motions of her ankle joint.

The podiatrist discovers that Mary rolls her feet inward as she runs. This rolling motion is probably causing the pains in her legs. Dr. Gordon decides to correct the problem by placing inserts in her shoes to control her foot motions. He makes plaster molds of Mary's feet, and sends them out to have plastic inserts, called orthotics, cast from the molds. Dr. Gordon expects that, when placed inside her shoes, the orthotics will prevent the rolling motion, and get rid of the pain.

Alex is a professional soccer player. He fractured his right leg during a game. Ever since the fracture mended, Alex has been working out at the Center. He wants to restore the strength in his right leg, and get back with his team. He is at the Center now to find out if he can start playing again.

The trainer seats Alex at a Cybex, a machine that measures muscle strength. As Alex raises a lever with his leg, the force he is applying is recorded on a strip of paper. The trainer keeps his eyes on the results. Soon he gives Alex the good news. His right leg is just about as strong as the other leg. He is ready to start working out with his team.

It is exactly one month since Dr. Torg operated on Donna's knee to remove some torn cartilage. She is in for her first checkup. Tina Bonci, a certified athletic trainer, uses a small, high-speed saw to cut open the thigh-to-toes cast. She is very careful not to nick Donna's leg with the sharp saw blade.

Once the cast is off, Tina cleans Donna's leg. She snips off the short lengths of surgical thread Dr. Torg used

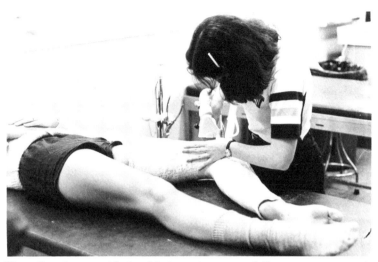

Tina Bonci, a certified athletic trainer, carefully removes Donna's cast.

(DR. JOSEPH S. TORG, SPORTS MEDICINE CENTER, UNIVERSITY OF PENNSYLVANIA)

to close the cut after the operation. Dr. Torg comes over and checks Donna's knee. He gives Tina a list of exercises that Donna should start doing in order to strengthen her leg muscles and the knee joint.

While on a winter vacation, Ted, a college senior, had a bad ice-skating accident. He completely shattered the bones of his right ankle. Dr. Torg operated, and inserted a metal screw to hold the bones in place while the ankle healed.

Dr. Torg looks at X rays of Ted's ankle, which had just been taken in the hospital across the street. He sees that the bones are mending well. He tells trainer Rick Berggren to remove the present cast, and replace it with a smaller one.

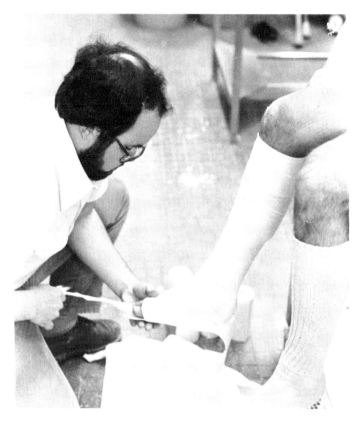

Certified athletic trainer Frederick Berggren is making a new cast for Ted.
(DR. JOSEPH S. TORG, SPORTS MEDICINE CENTER, UNIVERSITY OF PENNSYLVANIA)

To make the new cast, Rick takes lengths of cloth containing powdered plastic, and soaks them in a pail of water. Gently he arranges them around Ted's leg, making sure that the leg is in exactly the right position. He is also careful that the cast is neither too tight nor too loose. As soon as the wet plaster dries, it will form a solid, stiff cast.

Ted, an active athlete until his accident, has done almost no exercise for the last month. Rick, therefore, wants Ted to start getting back into shape. He gives him some exercises to get his heart and lungs working as they did before. Ted also gets a set of exercises for his thigh muscles and knee, which the old cast had kept locked in place.

As the stream of cases passes through the Center, the atmosphere remains cheerful and relaxed. Dr. Torg sets the tone. Somehow he finds the time to joke with the patients, to calm those who are nervous or frightened, and even to tease the trainers and other doctors working with him.

Dr. Torg's accomplishments in sports medicine may be due to his background as a football player in high school and college, and his great love for all sports. Surely he has an excellent understanding of athletes and their needs.

Dr. Torg believes that the athletes under his care should know exactly what is wrong with them, how they are being treated, and what to expect in the future. His patients become involved in their own medical care. Their good attitudes then help to speed their recovery.

Joe Vegso, the trainer, once said, "Dr. Torg doesn't baby his patients. If anything, he's tough on them." Perhaps he is. But his patients do not seem to mind.

3
New Knee Surgery

Susan is a 20-year-old college student and an avid tennis player. Not long ago she came to the office of Dr. Dinesh Patel, an orthopedic surgeon and codirector of the Sports Medicine Clinic of Massachusetts General Hospital in Boston. She was frightened and in terrible pain. The previous day, in the middle of a game, Susan's right knee had suddenly locked in place. Would she ever be able to play tennis again? How long would she have to be absent from school?

The Examination

First, Dr. Patel questioned Susan carefully about the injury. "How did you get hurt?" he asked. "Did you twist

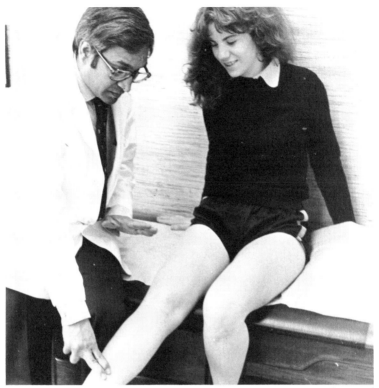

Dr. Dinesh Patel, co-director of the Sports Medicine Clinic of Massachusetts General Hospital, examines Susan after she hurt her knee playing tennis. (MASSACHUSETTS GENERAL HOSPITAL NEWS OFFICE)

your leg? Did you bang your knee? Did you fall down on it? Has this happened before?"

Susan told the physician how the accident had happened. She had twisted around quickly for a backhand shot. Suddenly she felt a sharp pain in her knee. That is when she fell. As she started to get up and tried to straighten her leg, the pain got worse. She found that she could not move the knee at all.

NEW KNEE SURGERY

From Dr. Patel's experience as a sports medicine doctor, as well as an amateur tennis player, he believed that Susan had probably torn the cartilage in her knee. The cartilage in the knee joint is made up of two half-moon-shaped wedges of tough, elastic tissue, called menisci, on either side of the knee. They serve as cushions or shock absorbers for the bones in the knee joint. They help to keep the joint stable. When the upper body twists without moving the foot, the cartilage can tear.

Torn cartilage in the knee is high on the list of common sports injuries. When it tears, cartilage does not heal. If the person is in pain or disabled, the only treatment is to remove the damaged cartilage by surgery.

Dr. Patel moved and bent Susan's knee in different directions. He carefully felt around the joint, looking for tenderness, swelling or other symptoms of injury. Step by step, he judged the extent of the injury.

When he finished this part of the exam, Dr. Patel ordered X rays of Susan's knee. He wanted to rule out a fracture or the unlikely chance that bone cancer or some other rare condition was causing the pain. After this, Dr. Patel called in Ara Sakayan, a registered physical therapist. Mr. Sakayan sat Susan at a Cybex machine to measure the strength, power and endurance of her good leg. Dr. Patel then set himself the goal of making

Susan's injured leg at least 90 percent as strong as the healthy one.

By now, Dr. Patel was quite convinced that Susan had indeed torn the cartilage in her right knee. But he took the time to talk to her and to get to know her better. Using a plastic model of the knee joint, he explained exactly what had happened inside her knee, and what he would advise to repair the damage. As a tennis player himself, he was able to make it very clear that he understood just how important the game was to her.

Dr. Patel proposed surgery to remove the damaged tissue. Further, he suggested an advanced new surgical method, called arthroscopy.

The name, arthroscopy, comes from the Greek. It literally means joint *(arthro)* seeing *(scopy),* or being able to see inside a body joint. The basic tool of this new kind of surgery is the arthroscope, a long, narrow (less than 1/5 of an inch or 6 millimeters wide), hollow tube like a metal drinking straw. The surgeon inserts the arthroscope into the joint, and can actually see the condition of the bones, lining, cartilage and ligaments inside. A number of different tools, similar in size and shape to this basic tool, can then be used to perform the many tasks necessary in knee surgery.

In order for Susan to understand the operation, Dr.

Patel took Susan to the audiovisual room in his office, and showed her a videotape made during previous arthroscopic surgery, explaining every step of the procedure.

Dr. Patel and Susan chose a date for the surgery. It would not be necessary for her to spend even one night in the hospital. She would arrive early that morning, be operated on that same morning, and return home late that afternoon. Further, before surgery, Mr. Sakayan would show her specific exercises so that she would not suffer any weakness in her legs.

The Operation

Susan could not help being a little frightened when she arrived at the hospital early on the day of the operation. But she had complete trust and confidence in Dr. Patel.

Susan was prepared for the surgery, and taken to the operating room. Here she was given a general anesthetic. The anesthetic made her unconscious; she would feel absolutely no pain during the surgery.

Dr. Patel started by making a small, quarter-inch incision, or cut, on the side of her knee. He inserted the arthroscope through the incision. A light shining through the tube allowed Dr. Patel to see inside the joint.

Dr. Patel, though, preferred to use a miniature, hand-

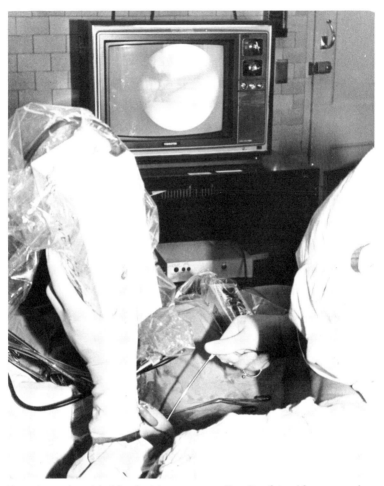

By using a hand-held television camera, Dr. Patel is able to see what is inside the knee on the monitor.

(MASSACHUSETTS GENERAL HOSPITAL NEWS OFFICE)

held TV camera that he attached to the outside end of the arthroscope. The greatly magnified picture appeared on a TV monitor in the operating room.

The closed-circuit TV offered several advantages. It

showed features inside the knee that might be hard to see in actual size. It let Dr. Patel work without craning his neck. The nurses and other staff were able to help more because they could see all that was happening inside the knee. Since he did not have to peer through the arthroscope, Dr. Patel kept his head away from the incision, lessening the chance of infection. And finally, Dr. Patel was able to videotape the whole operation for later study.

While holding the arthroscope and attached TV camera in one hand, Dr. Patel used his other hand to insert a probe through a second incision. With this probe he checked the bones, ligaments and cartilage inside the knee. He looked for any bits of loose material within the joint. As far as he could see, the only problem was the damaged cartilage.

Dr. Patel removed the probe and inserted a miniature instrument with a small, sharp knife blade at the end. Guided by the image of his movements on the TV screen, the surgeon deftly snipped off the torn section of cartilage. Dr. Patel's dexterity allowed him to handle the knife with either hand, while holding the TV camera with the other.

The physician next put a grabber, a sort of tiny plier, into the incision. He grasped the torn piece of cartilage and removed it from the knee. Next, he flushed the knee

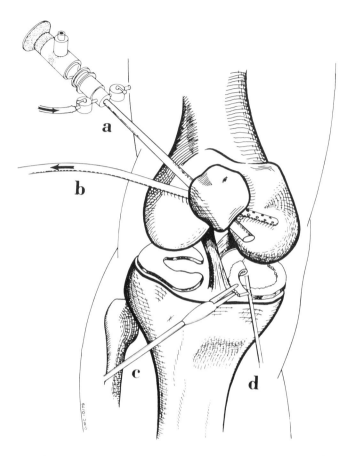

Dr. Patel uses four instruments during the operation: The arthroscope (a), a tube to remove fluids (b), a "grabber" (c), and a knife (d).

(MASSACHUSETTS GENERAL HOSPITAL NEWS OFFICE)

joint out with a saltwater solution to remove any loose particles and debris. Then, with a few stitches, he closed up the tiny cuts. The operation was over in less than half an hour. More difficult operations can take an hour or longer.

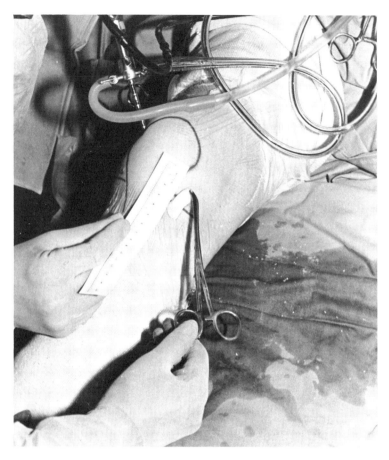

Dr. Patel measures the cartilage right after he has removed it from the knee. (MASSACHUSETTS GENERAL HOSPITAL NEWS OFFICE)

Susan was wheeled from the operating room to a recovery area. In a short while, the anesthesia wore off. Susan reported that she was feeling fine.

By late afternoon of the same day, Susan checked out of the hospital. Dr. Patel told her to walk with crutches to get extra support for her right knee.

The next day Susan was back at school. She began doing the knee exercises that Mr. Sakayan had shown her. Only ten days more and she was ready to play tennis again. Tests on the Cybex showed that over 90 percent of the original motion had been restored to her knee.

Although arthroscopy was the fastest, easiest way for Dr. Patel to remove Susan's torn cartilage, this method cannot be used for all knee surgery. Many knee operations can only be done in the more traditional way. This usually requires a longer incision, more destruction of tissue, a longer hospital stay, and an extended time for full recovery of the joint. Perhaps, in time, it will be possible to use arthroscopy more widely.

4
Keeping Athletes in the Game

Bobby Orr, an all-time hockey great, was on the All-Star team for five years, was voted Most Valuable Player three times, and broke all records for assists and scores by a defenseman. Yet he was always troubled by a failing left knee. At the age of 31, in the prime of his life, Orr officially retired as a player with the Boston Bruins. "I am no longer able to play," he told his many fans.

Star baseball pitcher Dizzy Dean won an astounding thirty-four games while playing for the St. Louis Cardinals in 1934. In 1937 he was hit in the toes by a line drive. The pain in his foot continued, and caused a body imbalance that threw off his delivery. The result was a serious arm injury that ended his career in 1941 at the age of 30.

There are many such tragic tales of athletes battling injury in professional sports. It is all part of the game, some say. But sports scientists are now working to change the situation. Many are devoted to helping top-level athletes give their best performance at all times. They care for the health needs of these players both on and off the field. They protect them from injury. And if the athletes do get hurt, they return them to peak condition as quickly as possible.

About 3,000 top-flight athletes are professionals in the United States today. They play on teams in baseball, football, hockey, basketball, and soccer leagues. And they compete as individuals in such sports as tennis, swimming, boxing, golf, and track and field.

A star player with a sprained ankle can cause a team to be eliminated from the league play-offs. A pulled muscle can mean the loss of a championship trophy. An athlete's injury can cause financial disaster for the player, or for his or her ball club. Some injuries can even dash an entire nation's hopes for success in an international match.

Caring for the country's athletes is a very weighty task. Sports scientists worry about the players they look after and are alert to any problems. A number have achieved remarkable results with prominent sports figures.

Dr. James A. Nicholas and the New York Jets

Dr. James A. Nicholas, an orthopedic surgeon, is the founder and director of the Institute of Sports Medicine and Athletic Trauma at Lenox Hill Hospital in New York City. Among other honors, Dr. Nicholas is a member of the President's Council on Physical Fitness and Sports, and was president of the Orthopedic Society for Sports Medicine. He is also the team physician for the New York Jets. In 1964, Dr. Nicholas performed the first reconstructive surgery on a football player's knee, actually rebuilding the badly damaged joint. When he performed similar surgery on football star Joe Namath the following year, Dr. Nicholas became world famous.

As the Jets team physician, Dr. Nicholas conducts preseason physical exams of all the team members. The main purpose of these general tests is to detect any weakness or other problem in the players' muscles and bones. When necessary, the doctor and his staff prescribe medical treatment, special exercises, or the use of such devices as braces or bandages to correct the trouble.

Dr. Nicholas, or another physician from the Institute, attends every Jets game. They are there to take charge in case there is any injury. When there is doubt about whether a player should continue playing after an injury,

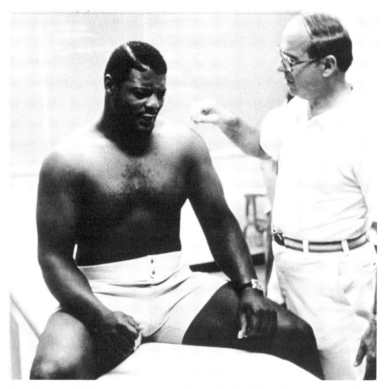

Dr. James A. Nicholas, team physician for the New York Jets, conducts
pre-season exams of the players.
(INSTITUTE OF SPORTS MEDICINE AND ATHLETIC TRAUMA, LENOX HILL HOSPITAL)

the team doctor helps to make that decision.

Every year the doctors at the Institute give physical exams to the hundreds of college players who are being considered for positions on the Jets. Each player is questioned about his medical history, with special attention paid to any old football injuries. He is also given a general physical exam, which includes testing the strength of his muscles and joints.

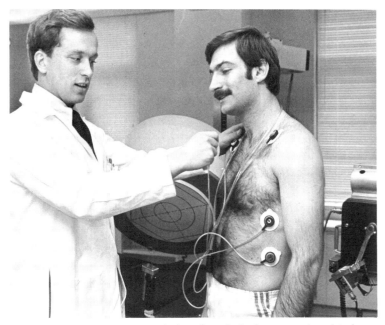

Electrodes are placed around the player's body to monitor his heart beat.
(INSTITUTE OF SPORTS MEDICINE AND ATHLETIC TRAUMA, LENOX HILL HOSPITAL)

An important part of the exam is the stress test. One of the workers in the Institute attaches electrodes around the player's body to monitor his heartbeat. A breathing mask is then placed over his mouth and nose to measure the amount of oxygen he is using. With all this equipment in place, the player is asked to run at a set speed on a treadmill. A treadmill is a platform with a wide belt that moves backward at a fixed speed. The person on the treadmill has to run at that speed to stay in one place. The various devices tell how well the player's body handles the stress.

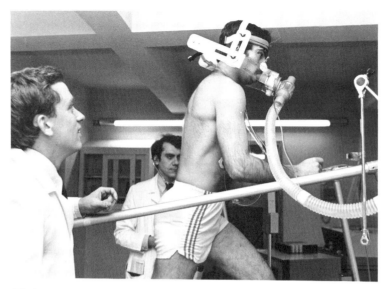

With electrodes and breathing mask in place, the athlete runs on the treadmill under the watchful eyes of the scientists. Automatic machines are monitoring his heart and his use of oxygen.

To test heart action, the player is injected with a substance that emits a small, entirely safe amount of low-level radiation. The man then lays down on a table, and a large gamma camera is placed over his heart. The camera is able to trace the movement of blood containing the radioactive material as it is pumped through the heart.

The doctor directs the player to do certain forms of exercise with his arms or legs. The TV screen connected to the gamma camera shows him how the flow of blood through the heart changes during exercise. This gives even more medical information about the fitness of the heart.

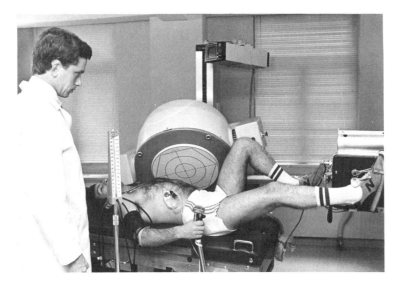

The athlete is under the gamma camera which measures the movement of blood through his heart as he pedals with his feet.

Usually, the coaches choose players for the team on the basis of talent and past performance. The Jets coaches, however, use the results to help them make up their minds when they have to pick between players with similar records.

Dr. Nicholas also uses these results. He compares the examination findings with the players' records. Is there any connection between factors, such as strength, weight, or lung capacity, and the player's achievements on the football gridiron? So far, Dr. Nicholas has not been able to foretell a player's abilities on the basis of the exam. But he hopes, one day, to have a test that will predict athletes' performances.

Another goal is to find relationships between certain health factors and the number of injuries a player will have during the season. Dr. Nicholas has found, for example, that players with loose, flexible joints tend to have more accidents than those with stiff, tight joints. Therefore, together with the team's trainers, he has worked out a series of exercises to strengthen the joints of players whose joints are too loose. The result has been a sharp drop in the number of injuries.

Dr. Frank Jobe and Tommy John

The date was July 17, 1974. The Los Angeles Dodgers were playing the Montreal Expos. At the top of the fifth, the Dodgers were leading, 4–0. Left-handed Tommy John was pitching for the Dodgers, going for his fourteenth win of the season. As he threw one pitch, he suddenly felt a powerful bang in his elbow. A sharp pain shot through his arm.

Dr. Frank W. Jobe, team physician of the Dodgers and cofounder of the National Athletic Health Institute in Inglewood, California, examined Tommy right away. He found that the pitcher had torn a ligament in his elbow. The ligaments are the strips of tissue that hold the bones together in the joints of the body. Pitching was out of the question. There was even doubt whether Tommy would ever regain the use of his arm at all.

Dr. Jobe decided to try a bold, new approach. He would substitute a length of tendon from elsewhere in Tommy's body for the torn ligament. Tendons, which connect muscles to bones, are made of a material almost identical to ligaments. He hoped it would work.

The operation that Dr. Jobe performed had two steps. First, he removed a length of tendon from Tommy's uninjured right arm, one that would hardly be missed. Dr. Jobe then drilled four holes in Tommy's left elbow and replaced the torn ligament with the strip of tendon.

The procedure went very well. But neither Dr. Jobe nor Tommy really believed that the arm would be strong enough for professional baseball. Dr. Jobe even advised Tommy to start thinking about a new career.

But Tommy refused to give up pitching. For two years, he worked very hard at building up his arm. Day after day he threw a ball against a wall, caught it, and threw it back again. Very slowly, the old strength and ability returned.

The pitcher went back to the majors. In 1976, he won ten games. In 1977, he won twenty. Starting in 1979 he played with the New York Yankees, reaching a peak of twenty-two wins in 1980. Sports writers began to call

After Dr. Frank W. Jobe rebuilt his injured left elbow, Tommy John became a star pitcher for the New York Yankees.

(NEW YORK YANKEES AND TOMMY JOHN)

him "the pitcher with the bionic arm." His success story attests to his personal courage and determination. It also points up the amazing skill of Dr. Jobe and the wonders of modern sports medicine.

Dr. John Marshall and Janet Newberry

In 1976, at the age of 24, Janet Newberry was one of America's leading tennis stars. Soon after winning an important match in the United States Open Tennis Tournament that year, Janet developed severe pains in her leg. Her doctor decided to operate. The operation, however, did little to relieve the pain. Her career was seriously threatened.

Finally, Janet went to see Dr. John Marshall, an outstanding sports physician. Dr. Marshall found that the problem was due to a weakness in the front muscles of her knee. Janet's kneecap, instead of moving up and down, shifted off to the side, which caused the pain.

Instead of prescribing rest or further surgery, the most common ways of treating this condition, Dr. Marshall decided to try a different approach. He set out to strengthen Janet's quadriceps, the front muscles of the thigh. Strong quadriceps would help to hold the kneecap in place, and prevent it from shifting to the side.

Janet worked out daily on a Cybex machine at the Hartsdale, New York, Fitness Center. Dr. Marshall chose Cybex because it allows a person to exercise muscles safely. The machine's resistance against Janet's leg adjusted at once to the force she was exerting. Thus she never could put too much strain on the muscles.

Dr. Marshall realized that Janet's style of playing tennis was making her condition worse. He spoke to her coach, Rick Ellstein, about changing the way she used her body during the game. The coach came up with a change in form which avoided too much stress on the knees. To take one example, if she bounced on the balls of her feet while waiting, rather than standing flat-footed in one place, she could return a shot faster and with less strain. He also showed her how to turn her body quickly without twisting at the knee.

Surgery had already proven useless. A period of rest would have only weakened Janet. But Dr. Marshall's method of strengthening her muscles and Rick Ellstein's help in improving her form solved Janet's knee problem *and* got her back into world-class competition. In 1977 she won the Italian Open, and was ranked among the world's top twenty players.

Dr. Richard Steadman and Phil Mahre

In March 1979, 21-year-old Phil Mahre was competing in the World Cup giant slalom on Whiteface Mountain at Lake Placid, New York. As he was going into the thirty-fifth gate, his ski slipped, he lost his balance, and he fell. The accident caused a four-part fracture of his left ankle and leg.

Dr. Steadman, who was head of the group of thirty physicians assigned to United States Olympic team athletes, advised an operation. In rebuilding the shattered ankle, Dr. Steadman found he had to insert a three-inch metal plate with seven screws to hold the fragments of bone in place.

Since Phil was a top athlete in excellent condition, the doctor started him on an exercise routine right after the operation. He gave Phil exercises for his upper body and uninjured right leg to maintain muscle tone and to keep his heart and lungs in good shape. For eight weeks, while Phil walked with crutches, he kept up with these exercises.

Gradually Phil was able to begin putting some weight on his left leg. Ten days later, he came off the crutches, and Dr. Steadman suggested he start bike riding. After four months Phil was able to water ski. In six months he entered his first race on skis, and came in second to his twin brother, Steve. Seeing that the bones had healed, Dr. Steadman was able to remove three of the screws.

Then, on February 22, 1980, Phil entered the slalom race at the 1980 Winter Olympics, and won the silver medal. This was doubly remarkable. No American had won a skiing medal of any kind since 1964. But more importantly, Phil had fully recovered in less than one year from an accident that would have surely ended his career if it had happened a few years earlier.

In April 1980, Dr. Steadman was able to take out the

metal plate and the remaining four screws. Phil's coaches say that his ankle has about 95 percent of the strength it had before the accident.

Dr. Gideon Ariel and Al Oerter

Four-time Olympic gold medal winner in the discus Al Oerter came to see Dr. Gideon Ariel at his Computerized Biomechanical Analysis company in Amherst, Massachusetts. Dr. Ariel holds degrees in computer science and exercise science. He also has an impressive sports background as a former discus thrower on the Israeli Olympic team.

Dr. Gideon Ariel shows discus thrower Al Oerter the computer model of his motions. (DATA GENERAL CORPORATION)

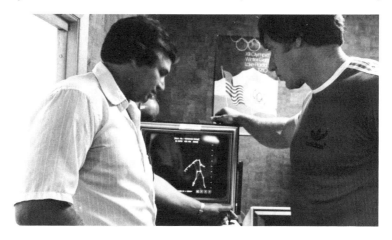

With Dr. Ariel's help, Al Oerter was able to improve his Olympic discus record. (PHOTO BY BRUCE BENNETT)

Oerter had retired after the 1968 Olympics, but wanted to make a comeback. Also, he hoped to improve on his best throw of 212.6 feet (64.8 m). At the time he came to see Dr. Ariel, though, he was only throwing 180 feet (54.9 m).

Dr. Ariel took some high-speed movie film of Oerter in action. He made a computer model of Oerter's motions while throwing the discus. The computer presented a stick drawing of Oerter's movements, and calculated the forces and speeds that he was using.

Oerter came to realize that in some ways he was not using his body correctly. He released the discus at the wrong angle. His full force was not going into the throw. The angle between his arm and body also did not give him the maximum leverage. Further, at the instant of release of the discus, both feet were not on the ground. This cut the distance he was able to throw.

Dr. Ariel gave Oerter exercises to strengthen his muscles, sharpen his timing, and improve his form. As a result, Oerter was able to raise his throwing distance to 221.4 feet (67.5 m). This is even better than Oerter's record set 14 years earlier. It is especially remarkable since Oerter was then 43 years old, usually thought to be quite old for discus.

5
Probing Sports Injuries

Sports scientists treat sports injuries. But they also work to *prevent* them. One of the first steps in checking these injuries is to learn as much as possible about sports accidents and what causes them. Important studies are now pointing out ways to stop accidents from happening.

All Sports

For one year, beginning in November 1974, a team of researchers from the Southern Illinois University School of Medicine, under Dr. Basilius Zaricznyj, took on the following task. They carefully studied all sports-related injuries of school-aged youngsters in the city of Springfield, Illinois. Complete records were kept on the number that were injured, the types of injuries, the sports that were involved, and how many accidents could have been prevented.

The scientists defined a sports injury as any accident that required first aid, a written report, or medical treatment. Injuries were considered serious if they either disrupted the body's structure, or damaged an organ. A fractured arm or a brain concussion are examples of serious injuries. Permanent injuries were those in which the body could not be restored to a normal condition. This included anything from a broken tooth to paralysis.

Dr. Zaricznyj and his team collected information from school principals and coaches, local physicians, hospitals and the schools' accident insurance company. Among the total school population of 25,512 during the year of study, they found 1,495, or 6 percent, sustained injuries. Boys aged 15 had the highest rate of injury, 15 percent. Girls peaked at age 14, when 8 percent were hurt. Overall, though, the boys had about twice as many injuries as the girls.

The probable explanation is that boys engage in high-risk sports, such as football, basketball and baseball, more than girls do. Boys also have a generally higher level of sports activity. Figures show, however, that when boys and girls participate in the same sport, the injury rate

Stickball is among the sports studied by the scientists at Southern Illinois University School of Medicine.

("THE SOUTHERNER," GREAT NECK SOUTH HIGH SCHOOL; PHOTO BY JON KLEIN)

About 38 percent of the injuries occurred in school physical education classes.

("THE SOUTHERNER," GREAT NECK SOUTH HIGH SCHOOL;

PHOTO BY ROBERT KOERNER)

is about the same.

Most of the injuries occurred to players in nonorganized sports. Forty percent of the injured were hurt during nonorganized and unsupervised sports activities.

School physical education classes ran a close second with 38 percent. Organized school sports accounted for only 15 percent of the injuries. The remaining 7 percent came from community team sports, such as Little League baseball. The sports that were responsible for the greatest number of injuries were football, 19 percent; basketball, 15 percent; gym games, 11 percent; baseball, 10 percent; and roller skating, 6 percent. Not only does the highest percentage of injuries occur in football, but football causes the most injuries, the majority of serious injuries, and the highest percentage of knee injuries.

Of all the injuries, 80 percent were considered nonserious; 20 percent were severe. Among those with serious injuries, 18 students, or 1.2 percent, had permanent disabilities. None of them, though, were left severely disabled.

The scientists reviewed each injury report. How had each accident happened?

Surprisingly enough, they found that slightly more than one out of every four accidents could have been avoided. Among the examples they cite are a swimmer falling from a diving board ladder and fracturing his skull, a brain concussion caused by a bat thrown during a baseball game, and a runner colliding with a fence and hurting his kidney.

Most accidents that could have been avoided took place

Basketball accounted for 15 percent of the injuries.

either during nonorganized sports or physical education classes. The key factor was carelessness. Dr. Zaricznyj and the others suggested that physical education teachers could help cut the number of injuries. They could spend more time teaching students safety habits common to all sports. Injuries will drop, the scientists said, when students begin to notice and avoid unsafe sports practices.

Youth Soccer

In many ways soccer is an ideal team sport. Soccer can be played on any open field or gym floor. The game requires no equipment beyond a ball and two goal nets. It can be played by people of any size or physical ability. An active sport, soccer provides lots of exercise for all of the players.

Soccer is rapidly growing more popular in America. A group of scientists at Oklahoma Children's Memorial Hospital did a study on the safety of the game. (WILLIAM A. GRANA AND RICHARD H. GROSS)

PROBING SPORTS INJURIES

Soccer has only caught on in America recently. As the sport has become more popular, more injuries related to soccer have come to the attention of the sports scientists. A team of doctors at the Oklahoma Children's Memorial Hospital of the Oklahoma University Health Sciences Center in Oklahoma City, therefore, decided to look into the safety of the game. They began to gather figures on the types of injuries incurred. These scientists kept track of the safety records of the 1,272 players, aged 7 to 18, during one season on teams in two leagues of the Frontier Country Soccer Association.

Once a week, the coach of each team telephoned the doctors with reports of any injuries. The scientists called an injury any medical problem that occurred during play that prevented the athlete from staying in the game.

By the end of the year they had a total of 34 injuries. Half of all the injuries were major; that is, the player missed more than 7 days of practice or games. The rate of injury was 7.7 per 100 in the older age groups (14 to 19 years old), but only 0.8 per 100 for the younger players (ages 8 to 14). The rate for girls was twice as great as for boys. This was exactly the opposite of the figures for all sports as shown in the Springfield study.

The most common injuries were sprains and bruises. The causes were equally divided between running, kicking

The goalie is the player most frequently injured in youth soccer.
(WILLIAM A. GRANA AND RICHARD H. GROSS)

and collisions. Six of the 34 injuries were to goalkeepers. Although goalkeepers make up only 6 percent of all soccer players, they received nearly 18 percent of all the injuries. This shows that goalie is the most dangerous position in soccer. The two main risks for goalies are being kicked or struck by a player on the offensive team, or hurting themselves when diving to stop a ball from reaching the goal.

Compared to other popular sports, the risk of injury to youngsters in soccer is less than half the rate for football players of the same age. It is about the same as for basketball.

The main findings of this study are clear. Although the injury rate in youth soccer is not significantly lower than other sports, the injuries are not serious. None led to a permanent disability. Therefore, the researchers decided, soccer is a safe sport for children and teenagers.

Football

About 1,200,000 players take part in high school, college and community football every fall. Most everyone agrees that there is a big risk of injury in this sport. Some of the most disabling of these injuries are to the head and neck. Sports medicine physician Dr. Joseph S. Torg set out some years ago to find the causes of these injuries. He was seeking ways to prevent head and neck injuries from occurring.

In September 1975, Dr. Torg was director of the Temple University Center for Sports Medicine and Science in Philadelphia. He began keeping records of football injuries in the states of Pennsylvania and New Jersey. During only the first month of that season, he learned of the following incidents:

Case 1. On September 1, a 17-year-old tackle on a high school team was injured while practicing with a spring-loaded tackling dummy. In this device a dummy

More than 1 million players take part in high school, college and community football. (CORNELL UNIVERSITY; PHOTO BY JON CRISPIN)

shoots forward with the force of a 300-pound man. The idea is for the player to tackle the dummy.

This time, though, the dummy struck the young player in the head, right where the face mask is attached to the helmet. While he was not knocked unconscious, he was thrown to the ground. At the same time, he lost all feeling in his arms and legs; they just went numb. Hospital X rays showed that he had fractured a number of disks in his upper spine.

Case 2. On September 13, a 13-year-old boy on a Midget League football team made a tackle, hitting the runner with the top of his helmet. The impact caused a fracture and dislocation of a disk in his upper spine that left him paralyzed in both arms and legs. Fortunately, an operation was able to correct the damage. The boy regained the use of his limbs.

Case 3. Later that month, a 17-year-old player was knocked unconscious when he was struck in the head by a spring-loaded blocking dummy during football practice. Despite intensive care in the hospital, he did not recover consciousness. He died two days later. An autopsy showed severe brain damage.

Altogether, Dr. Torg learned of twelve severe head or neck injuries during the 1975 football season just in the two states he covered. Of these, eight remained paralyzed and one died.

As a first step, Dr. Torg recommended that the use of spring-loaded tackling and blocking dummies be stopped at once. And secondly, he helped to set up the National Football Head and Neck Injury Registry to collect more data on players hurt in football games.

The National Athletic Head and Neck Injury Registry, as it is now known, began by inspecting players' records for the five years from 1971 to 1975. Of the 1.5 million players probed, 295 had suffered spine fractures or dislocations. Ninety-nine of them were left permanently paralyzed. Nineteen died.

Dr. Torg and the others looked carefully at these reports to try to learn the causes of these accidents. The greatest problem seemed to be that some players were using their helmets as battering rams. They tackled or blocked with their heads lowered, which straightened the upper part of the spine. Then they hit their opponents with the top of the head, in a motion called spearing. The huge force of the impact on the straightened spine brought about the accidents.

Dr. Torg passed along his findings to those who control high school, college, and professional-level football. Action came very quickly. Rules were passed forbidding players from using their heads and helmets to butt or spear other players. Coaches were strongly advised not to use mechanized tackling and blocking dummies.

The National Athletic Head and Neck Injury Registry has published its figures through 1977. They show a decrease in the number of serious football injuries on both the high school and college levels:

	1975	1976	1977
Head Injuries			
high school	18	18	9
college	2	2	1
Spine Injuries			
high school	68	95	65
college	23	20	16
Deaths			
high school	12	15	6
college	0	0	0

Most experts expect research to lead to further drops in the number of victims of such accidents.

6
The Body
as a Machine

Sports scientists have long believed running to be the most puzzling of all sports motions. The movements of runners' limbs are simply too fast and complex for the human eye to follow. The forces and pressures of the running body are very difficult to measure. Experts had no way to answer such questions as: How does a runner's foot strike the ground? What is the difference in stride between good and poor runners? What are the pressures on a runner's foot? Which running shoes protect best against injury? How can runners better their style?

A new science has begun to answer these and many other questions. It is called biomechanics, the study of the human body as a machine. Basically, it views arms and legs as mechanical levers that either apply force or

THE BODY AS A MACHINE

feel pressure. Recent advances in computers, high-speed movie cameras, and other electronic devices have extended our senses. They have made it possible for researchers to see and measure things that were once impossible.

Scientists make high speed films of a golfer's stroke in the Biomechanics Laboratory of Pennsylvania State University.

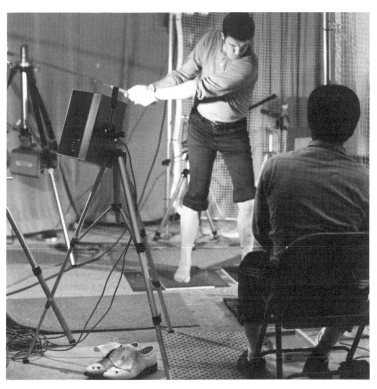

SPORTS MEDICINE

One of the leading biomechanical research laboratories is at Pennsylvania State University, University Park, Pennsylvania. The laboratory is under the direction of Peter R. Cavanagh, Ph. D., who is also a professor of biomechanics at the University. Dr. Cavanagh is well known in the field for his valuable research efforts. Many people know the name because of his yearly ratings of all the running shoes available. These ratings compare the different brands of shoes on the basis of how well they absorb the shock of the runner's feet striking the ground. Other considerations are the weight, flexibility, stability, and traction of the shoes, and how long they will wear.

Dr. Peter R. Cavanagh, kneeling, chats with leading marathon runner Bill Rodgers after testing him in the Biomechanics Laboratory of Pennsylvania State University.

(DR. PETER R. CAVANAGH, BIOMECHANICS LABORATORY,

PENNSYLVANIA STATE UNIVERSITY)

THE BODY AS A MACHINE

Comparing Distance Runners

In 1977, Dr. Cavanagh reported the results of a biome-chanical study on 22 distance runners. The runners were divided into two groups. Fourteen were top, or elite, runners, with an average speed for the marathon (26.2 miles [40 km]), of 2 hours, 16 minutes. Eight were good runners, not quite in the elite class. Their marathon speed averaged 2 hours, 35 minutes.

Olympic marathon champion Frank Shorter runs on the treadmill during an experiment at the Biomechanical Laboratory.

(DR. PETER R. CAVANAGH, BIOMECHANICS LABORATORY, PENNSYLVANIA STATE UNIVERSITY)

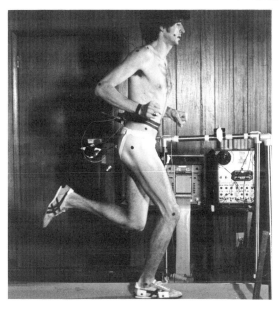

Dr. Cavanagh took high-speed motion pictures of the runners on a treadmill. He used an extremely fast camera that shot one hundred frames per second. This speed was needed to follow the runners' rapid movements. Dr. Cavanagh filmed the athletes from the side and from the front, running at several speeds.

Before the filming, small circles, known as target markers, were drawn on the runners' shoes, ankles, knees, thighs and hips. These markers would later be used for making precise measurements when viewing the film.

Each runner was photographed for 10 strides. The processed film was then projected down onto a flat surface, instead of onto a screen as in movie theaters. Beneath the surface was a built-in computer. As each frame appeared on the surface, a lab worker slid an electronic pointer to each target marker on the runner's body. By pressing a button on the pointer, the location of the spot was entered into the memory of the computer. In this way, frame by frame, the movements of each marker went into the computer.

The computer brought all of the figures together. As Dr. Cavanagh studied the columns of numbers, he noticed that the elite and good runners were very much alike. Only in stride length, which is the distance between ground contacts of the left and right feet, did they differ.

The lab worker enters the positions of the spots on the runner's body into the memory of the table computer.

Elite runners tended to have shorter strides than the good runners. The elite runners also had a higher stride rate, which is the number of steps per minute.

	Stride Length	Stride Rate
Elite	5.12 feet (1.56 m)	191
Good	5.38 feet (1.64 m)	182

Dr. Cavanagh also came upon some other "minor differences" in style between elite and good runners. But he warns runners not to try to change their style to match that of the elite runners. Most runners find the style that works best for them. They gain nothing by trying to imitate others, he says.

Dr. Cavanagh's study is typical of today's biomechanical research. It is not a major breakthrough in knowledge or understanding. Rather it just adds one or two pieces to the large jigsaw puzzle of the human body in motion. As Dr. Cavanagh put it, "Each study adds a fraction of one percent to the overall picture—a picture we desperately need more pieces to complete."

Forces on the Foot While Running

For years Dr. Cavanagh tried to find out exactly what happens at the point of contact between the foot and the ground. Finally, in 1980, he succeeded. Dr. Cavanagh devised an experiment that measured the forces on the foot as it struck the ground during distance running.

The scientist's main tool for this type of research is a force platform. This is a flat pad that electrically senses the pressure at hundreds of points across the surface. When someone steps on the force platform, the pressure causes a flow of electricity at the points of contact. The greater the pressure, the greater the electrical flow.

A connected recording device then produces a graph. The printout shows just which part of the foot strikes

A force platform is used to measure the pressures of a runner's foot on the ground. (DATA GENERAL CORPORATION)

first, the force of the contact, and the changing pattern of forces while the foot is on the ground.

Dr. Cavanagh placed the force platform on the floor near the center of a large room. Seventeen runners, male and female, with an average age of 24, took turns running past the force platform at a speed of about 6 minutes a mile (4 minutes per km), a common speed in distance running. They were told to run so that their right foot would land on the force platform as they went by.

All the runners were moving at about the same speed. Yet, each one produced a different pressure pattern. And none of them showed the expected pattern.

Most experts believed that distance runners touch the ground first with the heel. Dr. Cavanagh's study proved otherwise. In all cases, the first ground contact was made with the outside edge of the foot. This contact, though, ranged from the side of the heel forward to the side of the midfoot. Then, once the foot was on the ground, the center of force moved from the edge of the foot to the midline. Also, from the rear or middle toward the toes.

These findings are being used in two ways. For sports scientists working to prevent injuries, studies of the normal forces on the foot help them notice abnormal foot strikes. Now they are better able to search out connections between poor strikes and injuries.

A typical distance runner in training runs about 80 miles (130 km) a week, and has about 40,000 foot strikes in that time. Since the forces on the foot while running are up to twice that of walking, a minor problem in foot strike can lead to a major injury.

Shoe manufacturers are also applying this research to improved running shoes. Makers of running shoes can now base their designs on the facts and figures coming from the laboratories of scientists such as Dr. Cavanagh and other workers in biomechanics. Many of the new shoes are scientifically correct. They are tailored to the needs of the runners who will be wearing them.

Older shoes, to take one example, had padding only to protect the runner's heels. This is because it was

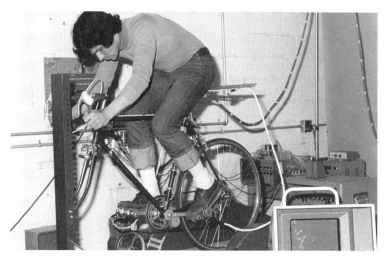

While the subject pedals the bicycle, a computer measures the forces that are applied. (DR. PETER R. CAVANAGH, BIOMECHANICS LABORATORY, PENNSYLVANIA STATE UNIVERSITY)

thought that the heel was the point of impact. Now that Dr. Cavanagh has shown that the side of the shoe strikes first, manufacturers are putting padding into the side of the shoe as well. He has also shown that the strong forces are felt all along the length of the shoe. Therefore, this padding now extends from the heel past the middle in the latest running-shoe designs.

Slowly, but surely, the work goes on. The scientists in biomechanical labs are doing experiments and gathering more information on the human body in motion. Already many sports are safer and many athletes are performing better because of the findings of these scientists. And we can be sure of even greater contributions in the future.

7
Matching People to Sports

People often turn to sports scientists for help and advice in choosing a sport. They ask: Which sport is best for me? Can I ski with a bad knee? Should I play baseball if I have tennis elbow? Will swimming build up my leg muscles? Am I too young to play football? Am I too old for basketball?

In the past, the scientists found it hard to answer these questions. There were few facts, based on research, to guide them in giving advice.

Experts have now found a way to match up people and sports. It is based on a 1977 study done by Dr. James A. Nicholas of the Institute for Sports Medicine and Athletic Trauma at Lenox Hill Hospital in New York City.

People often ask, "Which sport is best for me? Is it running . . .

. . . or is it gymnastics?"

Performance Traits

Dr. Nicholas first prepared a list of sixty-three sports, from archery to wrestling. Then he itemized twenty-one traits that contribute to success in sports. He covered physical traits, such as strength and speed, mental characteristics, such as intelligence and discipline, and other factors, such as practice and equipment.

Finally, Dr. Nicholas set out to learn which traits were linked to each sport. His object was to be able to steer people to the sports that best matched their strengths and abilities. In this way they could expect to enjoy the sport even more, and also to avoid injuries.

Dr. Nicholas considers the strength needed by a pole vaulter.
(CORNELL UNIVERSITY; PHOTO BY JON GRISPIN)

He takes into account the speed of the hurdle racers.

(PHOTO BY SUSAN BUREY)

Very early on, Dr. Nicholas made an amazing discovery. Physical traits are not most important. True enough, soccer players should have speed, football players should have strength, and distance swimmers should have endurance. But athletes who are slightly weak in some physical traits may be able to overcome the deficiency and still succeed. The five key traits that he did find necessary for success in most sports are: timing, accuracy, discipline, coordination and practice.

Good timing has two parts. One is to start the motion at exactly the right moment. The other is to bring together all the parts of the motion in the proper order and at the correct speed. Batting in baseball is an example of the need for good timing. The batter must start the swing at precisely the correct time to hit the ball properly. And

How important is practice for success in sports?

("THE SOUTHERNER," GREAT NECK SOUTH HIGH SCHOOL)

then the batter must follow through smoothly in order to add power to the hit.

Accuracy means being exact and precise in performing the motions of the sport. In tennis it is hitting the ball so that it lands exactly on the spot you are aiming for.

Batting in baseball shows the great importance of good timing.

(CORNELL UNIVERSITY; PHOTO BY JON CRISPIN)

In diving it is striking the water in just the right position. In basketball it is tapping a rebound directly into the basket.

Good athletes are able to control their impulses and desires. They direct all of their energy towards reaching their sports goal. Dr. Nicholas calls this discipline. Athletes with good discipline do not try to be stars, but work for the good of the team. They do not break training rules, no matter how great the temptation. They try to stay in top shape and be as sharp as possible at all times. And when they play, all of their attention is on the game.

Coordination, Dr. Nicholas says, is the ability to combine simple motions into more complex ones. The limbs and bodies of athletes with good coordination work together smoothly to accomplish the necessary movements of the sport. The motions and the senses are well coordinated, too. The hockey player used his legs to skate and handles the stick with his hands and arms; the pole-vaulter strains every muscle to clear the bar; the baseball pitcher stares at the catcher's mitt while going through the pitching motion.

Success in sport depends, too, on practice, on doing the required movements of the sport over and over again. In some ways, practice is the most important of all the traits. There is no athletic trait or skill that cannot be improved by practice.

The Motions of Sports

In his study, Dr. Nicholas also took a close look at motions used in the various sports. Hundreds of different motions were involved. Yet Dr. Nicholas found that they all fit into six large groups.

Throwing is the most common group of motions used in sports. Overhand, underhand, and sidearm are variations of the same motion. But as Dr. Nicholas points out, catching a baseball or football, hitting the ball in tennis or the puck in hockey, swinging a bat or golf club, as well as the shotput and basketball push-through, are closely related. Each of these uses the same body motions and makes similar demands on the body.

Almost every sport requires the player to hold some

Dr. Nicholas points out that hitting the puck in hockey is really a throwing motion.   (CORNELL UNIVERSITY; PHOTO BY JON CRISPIN)

Jumping is the third most popular motion in sports.
("THE SOUTHERNER," GREAT NECK SOUTH HIGH SCHOOL)

Kicking is the same motion as throwing, except that it uses the leg instead of the arm. ("THE SOUTHERNER," GREAT NECK SOUTH HIGH SCHOOL)

particular stance or position. The stance helps the athlete make the necessary motions. It also protects the body against injury. The racer's crouch, the football linesman's stance, the standard boxing position—all are necessary to do well in the sport.

The third most popular motion in sports is jumping. In jumping, the legs move the body up and forward off a surface. The jumping motion takes many forms too, from the broad jump and pole vault to the slide used in baseball.

The kicking motion is like throwing. The only difference is that the athlete uses the legs instead of the arms to propel a ball or other object away from the body. Football and soccer players have a number of different ways to kick, but the basic approach stays the same. Swimmers also use a variety of kicking motions to help them move through the water, but the movements resemble those of other sports.

Oddly enough, running only ranks fifth on Dr. Nicholas' list of most common sports motions. Running is like walking, except that there is some time when both legs are off the ground. Mostly used in racing, of course, running is part of such sports as basketball, baseball, soccer, tennis, and volleyball. Ice and roller skating also use the same general body movements.

The least used motion in sports is walking. In fact, archery, bicycling, fencing, polo, racing and swimming do not use walking at all. As common as walking is to daily life, it is a seldom used motion in sports.

Putting It All Together

Having divided all sports motions into the six types, Dr. Nicholas then asked the question: Which sports demand the most motions from athletes?

The difference between running and walking is that both legs are off the ground at the same time when you run.

(PHOTO BY SUSAN BUREY)

To get the answer, Dr. Nicholas set up a rating system. Each sport got six separate numbers, one for each motion. If the sport demanded little or no use of a particular motion, he gave it a zero. Mild use earned a one, moderate use a two, and heavy use a three. The sum of the six numbers then tells the demands that sport puts on the player.

Swimming, for instance, rates zero for walking, running, and jumping. But heavy use of kicking gives it three points, heavy use of the throwing motion, three points, and moderate use of stance, two points. The overall motion score for swimming is eight points.

The highest score for any sport is 18. None score that

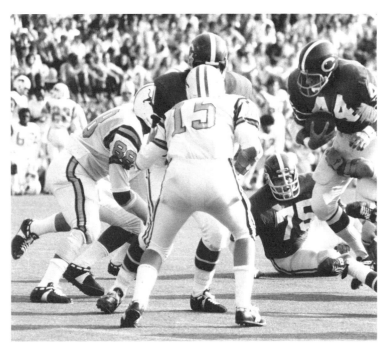

Football is one of the highest scoring sports according to Dr. Nicholas's system, with 15 points.

(CORNELL UNIVERSITY; PHOTO BY RUSSELL HAMILTON)

high, though. Basketball, football, skiing and soccer score the highest with totals of 15 points. Next, with scores from 12 to 15, are baseball, diving, figure skating, gymnastics, hockey, rugby, tennis and volleyball.

Sports with scores from 9 to 11 include badminton, lacrosse, surfing, tumbling and wrestling. Finally, the 5 to 8 group takes in archery, bicycling, bowling, calisthenics, canoeing, golf, hiking, racing (running), scuba diving, swimming and table tennis.

Dr. Nicholas' research is proving to be a valuable tool.

Wrestling is ranked between 9 and 11 points.

(CORNELL UNIVERSITY; PHOTO BY JON CRISPIN)

Sports scientists, physicians, coaches and trainers all use his charts. It helps them to suggest sports for individuals who seek help in making a choice.

With the chart, they can compare the demands of each sport with the strengths and disabilities of anyone who wants to play. They can suggest the sports that offer the best chance of success and enjoyment, and the least danger of injury. Given the demands of each sport, they can plan training routines to help people stay in sports they like best.

8
Improving Sports Performance

Just before the 1976 Winter Olympics, one cross-country skier was performing so badly that he was expected to be a failure in his event. At the Games, though, he came close to getting the best time of all the competitors in his part of the relay race. His success moved the United States team from twelfth to eighth place.

In midseason, a varsity high school basketball player lost her confidence because she wasn't making any of her shots. After only a few days, she was playing as well as ever, and went on to lead her team to win the league trophy.

A placekicker on a college football team was nearly perfect at practice. During games, though, he missed several game-winning kicks. One season later, this kicker was doing as well at the games as at the practice sessions. In fact, he set a national record for the longest kick in college football.

In each case, a sports scientist turned things around for the player. How was the change made? Not by bettering the athlete's physical condition, but by improving his or her mental state. The scientists who helped these players are called psychologists. These experts are specialists in human behavior. Those who deal mostly with mental aspects of athletes and athletics are known as sports psychologists.

Sports Psychology

Dr. Richard M. Suinn of Colorado State University, Fort Collins, Colorado, is an outstanding sports psychologist. He has been the team psychologist for the U.S. Nordic ski team at the 1976 Winter Olympics, and for the Women's Track and Field team at the 1980 Summer Olympics. He is best known, though, for helping athletes overcome stress and nervousness. This lets them perform at their peak.

Dr. Suinn teaches the athletes to relax the various muscle groups of the body through a method of progressive relaxation. In this system, Dr. Suinn first shows the athlete

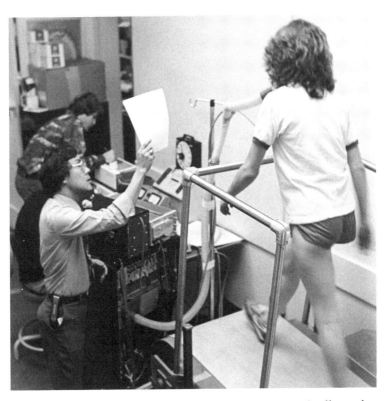

Dr. Suinn holds up a card telling an athlete on a treadmill to relax.
(COLORADO STATE UNIVERSITY OFFICE OF PUBLIC COMMUNICATION
AND RICHARD M. SUINN)

how to feel both tension (tightness) and relaxation (looseness). He seats the player in a comfortable chair, and instructs him or her to raise a wrist and make a very tight fist. This creates a tension in the arm and hand. Then he tells the athlete to open the fist, relax, and let the hand rest on the chair.

"Can you feel the difference?" Dr. Suinn asks the player.

Most can easily feel the change. Then Dr. Suinn teaches them to create tensions and relaxation in different muscles around the body. After a short period of training, the athletes do not need any more help. They are able to relax their muscles at will, even before stress.

Dr. Suinn has another plan to improve athletic performance. It is called visuo-motor behavior rehearsal, or VMBR, for short. This approach to training has three basic steps.

The first is to give the athletes lessons in progressive relaxation. The next step is for the player to call to mind mental images of the sport. Dr. Suinn calls this "body thinking." The goal is to create vivid images of taking part in the sport. Swimmers feel the water on their skins, and smell the chemicals in the pool. Skiers see the slope in front of them, and hear the wind whistling as they speed along. Runners sense the buildup of tension before the race, and the burst of energy as the starter's gun explodes.

Lastly, the athlete mentally rehearses the skills of the sport, while seated calm and relaxed. The ice skater adjusts her body balance as she goes through her figures. The pitcher winds up and throws a fastball smack into the center of the catcher's mitt. The football halfback twists and turns while running for a goal with the ball.

Before one major race, gold-medal skiing champion Jean-Claude Killy could not practice on the slopes because of an injury. The only way he could prepare for the race was through the use of mental imagery. Killy later reported that it was the best race he ever skied!

By now, a number of other psychologists have adopted Dr. Suinn's approach. Through progressive relaxation and VMBR, they have helped many athletes. Players report sharper skills, increased confidence, and improved performance.

Still, there is little hard scientific evidence that the system works. It is very difficult to carry out experiments to prove that athletes really get better as a result of sports psychology.

Dr. Suinn's first experimental study of VMBR shows what can happen with such tests. Dr. Suinn divided the Colorado State University ski team into two groups that were about equal in size and ability. He gave one group VMBR training; the other group got only the ordinary training.

The VMBR group, though, improved so much that it actually ruined the experiment. The coach would not allow members of the untreated group to take part in the events. This made it impossible to compare results. But the fact that the VMBR group won the league trophy

IMPROVING SPORTS PERFORMANCE

and got many individual honors surely points up VMBR's usefulness.

Wanting to Win

To do well at sports, an athlete needs special skills and talents for the game. But what is also important is a strong will to excel, sometimes called sports motivation.

Dr. Dorcas Susan Butt of the University of British Columbia, Vancouver, Canada, has a special interest in sports motivation. Once she was a champion tennis player. Now she is well known as a sports psychologist.

Sports psychologist Dr. Dorcas Susan Butt was a champion tennis player before turning to psychology.   (PHOTO BY CHRIS GALLAGHER)

Part of Dr. Butt's time as a sports psychologist is spent just talking with athletes.   (PHOTO BY JOHN MORRIS)

Dr. Butt finds that an athlete's motivation stems from a number of different basic drives. Her main research goal is to understand and explain the various types of athletic motivation. She is also trying to discover which of the motivations are most helpful to the athlete's personality.

According to Dr. Butt, there are four levels of sports motivation. The basic level is the life force. This biological energy, she says, is part of every human's drive to live and will to win.

The next level are the psychological motivations. They

are aggression, conflict and competence. All three of these motivations may be present in the same athlete. Usually, one of them is stronger than the others, however.

Aggressive athletes have a great deal of energy. Much of this energy is directed against their opponents. They also tend to be very active and eager. Althea Gibson, the Wimbledon tennis champion in 1957 and 1958, is an example of an aggressive athlete. Miss Gibson always played a hard, strong game. She once said that she felt like attacking her opponents physically at times.

Conflict-motivated athletes are often unhappy and moody. They use sports to work out neurotic conflicts within their personalities. One young man who was well developed physically but very shy had a strong need to show himself off to others. He took up weight lifting as a way of improving his self-image. Ultimately he became an Olympic gold medalist.

Many of the top athletes, too, are motivated by the competence drive. These players perform to the best of their abilities because it fulfills their own inner needs. They are less interested in whether they win or lose.

Roger Bannister, the first runner to break the four-minute mile, was a competence-motivated athlete. He set himself high goals, and then worked to meet them. When racing, he was satisfied if he ran well, even if he did not win the race. In 1965, Bill Rodgers, a leading marathon runner, ran the mile in 4:18:8. Fifteen years later, "just to see if I could do it," he cut two seconds off his record.

Competition and cooperation make up the two social motivations. Competition, says Dr. Butt, is the "win at all costs" attitude. It springs from the aggressive and conflict motivations. Competitive athletes focus their attention on doing better than the others. Cooperation is just the opposite. It comes from the competence motivation. Cooperative athletes work well with others and put the team's success above personal gain.

Most individual sports, though, stress competition. To win, you have to beat, or do better than, someone else. But Dr. Butt believes that even here there is room for cooperation. Athletes can be friendly and helpful, even though they are working hard to win.

The final level affects both psychological and social motivations. Dr. Butt calls it the rewards of sports motivation. Part of this motivation comes from others. It includes praise, attention, prizes and status. But another very important part comes from within. It centers around such factors as pride, confidence, and a good sense of self.

Dr. Butt's findings are changing sports. They show

that competence and cooperation can improve an athlete's chances of succeeding in sports. Players with these drives are happy and fulfilled people. Competition and aggressiveness, which many athletes value so highly, may be bad for some athletes, and bad in some sports.

Improving sports performance and understanding motivation are only two lines of study in sports psychology today. There are many others. Among them are these:

Can psychological tests be used to predict athletic success? (One study showed that a standard test was 70 percent correct in picking those who would do well in Olympic competition; when combined with records of past performances and physical exams, it proved to be 90 percent correct.)

How can staleness in training be avoided? (Leave time between practice sessions, and don't overcoach.)

What is the psychological makeup of a typical athlete? (Athletes tend to be outgoing, enthusiastic, confident, aggressive, and have a strong will to succeed.)

Is there any value to the before-the-game pep talk? (It does not help; there seems to be more value in a talk after the game between athletes and coach.)

The one thing that all research in sports psychology does show—there is more to winning than just learning the rules of the game.

9
Sports Medicine and Drugs

Willis Reed of the New York Knicks ruptured a muscle in his right thigh during the 1970 National Basketball Association play-offs. The team physician gave Reed an injection of a painkiller so that he could keep playing. Reed played for twenty-eight minutes, long enough to assure the Knicks of victory. Later the physician said, "That was a situation where the game was for the world championship, and the fact that Willis really wanted to play."

Doctors found traces of amphetamines, or uppers, in the urine of the leading Dutch cyclist, Ad Tak, just before a six-day bicycle race. He was not allowed to participate. Many bicycle racers take drugs to help them in their grueling races. But most use other substances to remove

SPORTS MEDICINE AND DRUGS

traces of the amphetamines from their urine. One professional English cyclist said, "Ad was caught because his doctor goofed up."

The Bulgarian weight lifter Blagoi Blagoev had to give back the silver medal he won in the 1976 Olympics at Montreal. A routine test showed that he had used steroid drugs, which he believed made him stronger. Blagoev was like many other world-class weight lifters today. He felt that if he wanted to win, he needed to take these drugs.

Some athletes take drugs to control pain, to do better in competition, or to build up their strength. But sports scientists wonder: Do these drugs do what they are supposed to do? Are they safe? Should drugs be allowed in organized sports?

Painkillers

For professional athletes, pain is a fact of life. They often take painkillers because they want to keep competing despite pain or injury. Perhaps they are afraid of losing their position on the team. Sometimes they cannot resist the pressure from management, the fans, or other players to stay in the game even when they are hurting.

Doctors can inject players with local anesthetics, such

Pain is a fact of life for many athletes.   (PHOTO BY MELVIN BERGER)

as Carbocaine or Xylocaine, which produce numbness. They can also use anti-inflammatory drugs, such as cortisone, to lessen pain by reducing swelling. All painkillers permit injured athletes to play with injury. The results, though, are often not good.

A famous case concerns Bill Walton, a leading player with the Portland Trail Blazers in 1978, and Dr. Robert Cook, the team physician. In April, during an important play-off game, Dr. Cook injected Walton with painkillers, for what the doctor described as a "chronic condition."

Most players are able to take part in the bruising game of football without using pain killers. (CORNELL UNIVERSITY; PHOTO BY JON CRISPIN)

Fifteen minutes later, Walton had to leave the game. The pain had become too great. An X ray taken the next day showed Walton had broken a bone in his foot. The injury put him out of play for the entire next season.

Walton later said the injection had caused the bone to fracture. The physician denied any connection between the break and the injection. What is more, he let it be known that he gave the injection with the player's knowledge and consent.

Another physician, who later became Walton's agent, said that the injections caused numbness. This lack of sensation interfered with the athlete's natural reflexes. Without proper reflexes, a player is more likely to suffer injury. Indirectly, then, the injection may have caused Walton's fracture.

The doctors who give painkillers believe that not all such substances are bad. They say that painkillers are sometimes harmless and even helpful. Physicians who disagree doubt that painkillers are ever entirely safe. They argue that pain is a signal that something is wrong in the body. By blocking the signal with drugs, a player may do serious damage—and not even know that there is a problem.

Generally speaking, doctors are becoming more cautious. They tend to use local anesthetics and anti-inflammatory drugs much less. Many now think that large doses of these substances may cause serious side effects. The troubles range from ulcers and fever to death. But the question still remains: Are there *any* cases where painkilling injections should be allowed during a game or meet?

Amphetamines

Amphetamines are commonly known as uppers or pep pills. Many users believe that these drugs make them feel less tired, more energetic, and highly alert. They are

Most basketball players are able to play this exhausting game without using drugs. (CORNELL UNIVERSITY; PHOTO BY JON CRISPIN)

the drugs most often used by athletes.

Dr. Lawrence A. Golding, an exercise physiologist, did an important study on how amphetamines affect athletic performance. His subjects were twenty students at Ohio's

Kent State University during one track season. Ten of the subjects were runners on the University track team. The other ten were nonathletes.

The subjects were asked to run a number of times on a treadmill until they could run no more. Sometimes they were given amphetamines before they ran. Sometimes they were given placebos, harmless sugar pills that look just like the amphetamines. All the pills were marked with code numbers. Nobody knew until after the experiment whether the subjects were receiving amphetamines or placebos.

Twelve minutes after the students finished their first runs, they were asked to run again. In this way, Dr. Golding could see the effect of the amphetamine on both rested and tired runners.

Dr. Golding found that both groups could run slightly longer with the amphetamine than with the placebo. The tired runs for both groups were a bit shorter with the amphetamine. These differences, though, were not significant. It led to the conclusion that the amphetamines did not change performance.

Amphetamines, it is now known, may have bad effects. Football players on the drug feel tired and bruised as long as four or even five days after a game. Long-distance runners on uppers take twice as long to recover from a

SPORTS MEDICINE AND DRUGS

race as non-drug takers.

Amphetamines often make players hostile and aggressive. Some say that the most violent hockey players may be showing the effects of these drugs. Users also may lose their judgment. They think that they are doing better than they really are. And they cannot make fast decisions. Other symptoms include an irregular heartbeat, headaches, weight loss, upset stomachs and, in extreme cases, death. Dick Howard, the 1960 Olympic hurdler, and Tom Simpson, the English cyclist in the 1967 Tour de France race, both died as a result of amphetamine abuse.

Amphetamines do not improve performance, are habit forming, may cause serious side effects, and can even kill. They are condemned by all the major sports associations. Yet, they are still widely used. Why?

Some think it is because ours is a drug-oriented society. People have faith in "magic" pills. Sports physician Dr. Gabe Mirkin once asked one hundred leading runners whether they would take a pill that would get them an Olympic gold medal, but would kill them in one year. More than half said that they would take such a pill!

Psychological factors also play a role. If players believe that they will do better with amphetamines, it may help, even though the substance itself does nothing to improve their skills.

In 1964 Bob Bauman, trainer for baseball's St. Louis Cardinals, brought three bottles of pills into the locker room. The green pills, he told the men, would improve batting, the yellow pills would raise the number of runs batted in, and the green pills would help pitchers throw shut-out games.

As Bauman said, "Virtually every player on the team took them, and some wouldn't go out on the field until they took my pills. They worked so well that we won the pennant." Bauman used the pills for two more seasons, and the Cardinals won pennants both times.

What was the magic ingredient? There was none. The pills were placebos. They succeeded only because the players expected them to!

Anabolic Steroids

Second in popularity to the amphetamines are the anabolic steroids. Many athletes believe that they increase strength, weight, and endurance, and generally build up the body. Among a group of champion wrestlers, weight lifters, and other "strength" athletes, Dr. Golding found that most had taken or were taking steroids.

Anabolic steroids are male hormones. These chemicals from within the body are not well understood. But it is known that they help to produce some of the body characteristics that distinguish men from women.

Opinions are divided over the claims made for and against steroids. Research often produces conflicting results. Among a recent group of studies, four showed that steroids do not improve strength. One found weight increase. (Researchers believe this might be because steroids cause the body to retain water.) Five other studies, though, did show additions in strength and weight. And when the steroid was given along with a protein supplement in one study, the muscles grew larger.

Here, too, Dr. Golding ran his own careful experiment. The subjects were forty weight lifters who were told that they would be divided into four groups and given four different types of steroids and protein. Actually, the four groups received either steroid and protein, steroid and placebo, placebo and protein, or two placebos. No one knew which was which.

Before the study began, the athletes were examined. Measurements were taken of body size, muscle size, weight, proportion of fat, and strength in weight lifting. During the twelve-week-long experiment, they continued their usual training and diet routines. At the end of the time, all were measured and tested once again.

None of the four groups of athletes showed any great

changes in body measurements, muscle size or fat. All, however, showed some increase in strength. Several of the subjects were already taking steroids. Therefore, Dr. Golding believes that the strength gains were due to psychological, rather than physical, effects. Steroids, he says, do not significantly improve body weight, size or strength.

Why do the steroid results differ so widely? One theory is that only those who are training at their maximum gain from steroids. They are able to work even harder while taking the drug. The extra practice improves their strength, not the steroid itself.

The American College of Sports Medicine warns athletes to beware of the steroids. There is no real proof that they help performance, but a lot of evidence that they can be harmful. Men taking the steroids have developed serious sexual disorders. Women sometimes find themselves with male characteristics, such as hair on the face. And both sexes, on occasion, have suffered liver damage, nausea, acne and peptic ulcers.

The evidence of Dr. Golding and others argue against the use of any drugs in sports. Yet many sports physicians still believe in prescribing them. This has led someone to say: "If we are not careful, soon sports contests will be between doctors and the pills they prescribe, not between athletes."

10
Sports Medicine
and You

Sports medicine is a fast-growing field. About five hundred reports on new sports medicine discoveries are made every month. Sports doctors are developing new and better ways to prevent and treat sports injuries. Trainers, coaches, and physical therapists are learning ways to help athletes play better, enjoy the game more, and recover more quickly when they get hurt.

All athletes can benefit from these advances. Here's how some of the findings of sports medicine can help you.

Physical Fitness

Physical fitness, doctors say, is your ability to adapt well

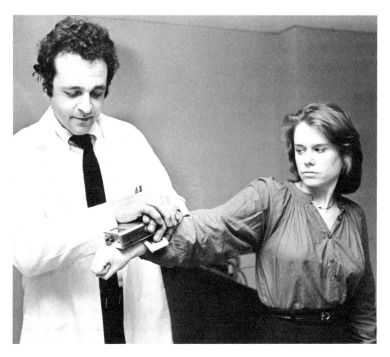

Dr. Barry Goldberg of the Institute of Sports Medicine and Athletic Trauma tests a new device to measure muscle strength.
(INSTITUTE OF SPORTS MEDICINE AND ATHLETIC TRAUMA, LENOX HILL HOSPITAL)

to physical effort. It depends on two sets of factors. One is your general physical condition, which includes how well your body is able to resist disease and injury. This side of fitness comes from minding the well-known rules of good health.

Physical fitness also involves the tone or condition of your muscles. Muscle tone refers to muscle strength. It also means muscle power, being able to produce a sudden burst of force. And it includes endurance, the ability to repeat a motion without tiring or weakening.

An athlete is being tested for muscle strength at the National Athletic Health Institute.

(NATIONAL ATHLETIC HEALTH INSTITUTE, CENTINELA HOSPITAL MEDICAL CENTER)

Your muscles are made of protein. Therefore, foods rich in protein, such as cheese, meat, fish, eggs and milk should be part of your daily diet. For a long time, sports experts suggested a meal of protein just before an important game, race or meet. Now they find a meal rich in carbohydrates, that is, bread, cereal, rice, potato and fruit, is much better. Carbohydrates are the fastest source of maximum muscle energy. You should eat this meal at least two hours before the game. This way it is mostly digested before you play.

Exercise helps to strengthen your muscles.   (PHOTO BY MELVIN BERGER)

To derive energy from the foods you eat, your muscles need a good supply of oxygen. The oxygen is brought to your muscles by the red blood cells. The way to increase the amount of oxygen reaching your muscles is to strengthen your heart, so that it pumps more blood with each beat. Exercises, therefore, that build up your heart muscle, will help all of your muscles to work their best.

Exercise has been a major subject of study by sports scientists. They are trying to answer the question most of us ask at one time or another, "How much exercise is best for me?"

Dr. Michael Pollock of Wake Forest University made some interesting findings. For example, he found out that you gain little by exercising more than five times a week.

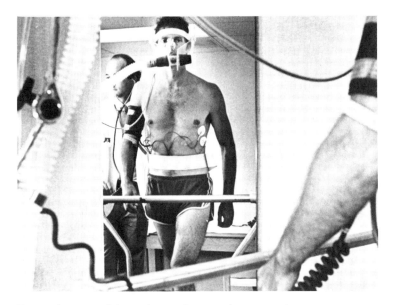

Researchers are doing advanced research on exercise.
(NATIONAL ATHLETIC HEALTH INSTITUTE, CENTINELA HOSPITAL MEDICAL CENTER)

Working out about three times weekly is probably best. In fact, when distance runners trained more than three days a week, the number of foot and leg injuries rose sharply. The body, it seems, needs time to rest and recover between periods of hard exercise.

Exercise also means planning the workouts so that you are in top form on the day of an important event. Making the muscles work harder and harder up to the moment of performance, scientists now know, can result in a loss in efficiency.

Many top athletes now follow a regular routine to build strength, power and endurance up until the last days before competing. Then they cut the time spent training.

For some it may mean training harder, but for shorter periods. A weight lifter may use heavier weights, but lift them fewer times. A baseball pitcher may throw fewer practice pitches, but throw them harder.

Kinds of Exercise

You can do hundreds of different exercises to help you become physically fit. Sports scientists divide them all into four basic types.

First, the nonresistance exercises. These are done without any extra load or resistance on the muscles. The most popular are push-ups and sit-ups, and sports such as swimming, running, and bicycling. Nonresistance exercises help your heart and lungs to work better. They lengthen and to some extent strengthen your muscles. Use them to warm up before hard exercise. For the greatest benefit, repeat the motions of these exercises as many times as you can, but with plenty of rest between sessions.

Among the resistance exercises are drills in which the muscles work against an object that does not move or give way. Such exercises are called isometrics. Pushing against a wall or trying to pull apart your clasped hands are examples of isometric exercises. Isometrics build up the size and strength of muscle in one position, but not throughout their whole range of motion. Isometrics do not lengthen muscles, either.

Lifting weights, or working out on machines where you can set the weight or resistance, are known as isotonic exercises. Here your muscles work against a fixed resistance, even though you can change the resistance by changing weights or adjusting the machine. The popular Nautilus machines provide isotonic exercise. Isotonics are widely used for building up the size and strength of muscles.

The latest resistance exercises are called isokinetic. Isokinetic exercise machines automatically and immediately adapt the resistance to the amount of force of your muscles. The Cybex is the most popular of the isokinetic machines. It has a lever which is set to move at a fixed speed. As you push on the lever with any part of your arm, leg or body, the lever always pushes back with the exact same pressure. Thus, you can exercise at your maximum strength without the risk of pushing too hard and injuring yourself.

Finding the exact exercises that are best for you, experts tell us, depends on your own fitness goals and the sports you like. Ask your coach, trainer or gym teacher to advise you on the exercises that will be of greatest value. Just keep in mind these five general rules:

Don't exercise hard every day; take hard days, easy days and rest days.

Work to your capacity, never beyond it.

Don't take long vacations from exercise or your muscles will soon lose their conditioning.

Plan your exercises so that you peak on the day of a game or meet.

Whatever your sport, try to practice the exact motions you need to play the game.

Good physical fitness is a wonderful goal. It will make you a better athlete and a healthier person.

Sports Injuries

Every one who takes part in sports knows about scrapes and bruises, sore muscles, and painful joints. Many also know about strains and sprains, tears and fractures. But did you know that sports scientists believe that 80 percent of all sports-related injuries can be prevented? Dr. Dinesh Patel of the Sports Medicine Clinic at Massachusetts General Hospital says that it is a matter of knowing the dangers and looking out for them.

Sports physicians group injuries by the structure that is affected, not by the sport. Muscle injuries are the most common. When you work your muscles to the maximum, you may get muscle soreness. This is a signal that those muscles need some time to rebuild themselves. If you actually overload your muscles, you may get what is called a pulled muscle. This is a tear or rupture of some of the muscle fibers. The symptom is a sharp, sudden pain in one area, which does not go away.

A muscle cramp is a painful tightening of a muscle. Often it is due to a lack of essential minerals, such as potassium or magnesium, in your diet. The simple treatment is to add more fruits, vegetables, and grains to your intake of foods.

Weak, stiff muscles suffer more injuries than strong, flexible ones. In fact, stiff muscles are believed to cause eight out of ten sports injuries. A warm-up period spent loosening and stretching tight muscles is considered vital for all athletes before any sports activity. Oddly enough, the more fit you are, the greater your need for these warm-ups. Muscles that are in good condition tend to be strong and tight. Consequently they require the most preparation before physical effort.

The tendons of the body are also often subject to sports injury. When you put a great deal of strain on the tendons they may become inflamed. A painful condition known as tendonitis results. An athlete that suddenly and violently contracts a muscle may tear the tendon holding that muscle to the bone. When this happens, he or she usually hears a pop and feels severe pain.

A strong blow or too much pressure on a bone may cause the bone to fracture or break. A stress fracture is only a slight crack in the surface of the bone. In a complete fracture the bone is actually broken. Bones, though, heal themselves. Usually the doctor lines up the parts of the broken bone and puts a cast over the area. This insures that the bone cannot move and will mend properly.

Lastly, the joints of the body sustain a large number of injuries. The knee joint is hurt most often, although the shoulder, elbow, ankle and wrist are also damaged at times. Different bones come together in the joints. The ends of the bones are lined with cartilage, and are kept in place by the ligaments. A blow, twist, overuse or too much push or pull on a joint can harm the cartilage or sprain or tear a ligament. Pain, swelling and sometimes an inability to move are the usual symptoms of joint injury.

What do the scientists advise athletes to do in case of sports-related injuries?

The first step, they say, is to decide if it is a serious injury. Severe pain is usually a warning of severe injury. Even mild pain that does not go away for a period of time may signal serious trouble. Any injury to a joint is serious. And, in general, if you are worried about an injury, there is a good chance that it is serious.

All serious injuries, of course, should be seen and treated by a professional. In some cases, it means telling your coach or trainer about the pain and getting advice on what to do next. At other times, it means going directly to a sports medicine clinic, a local doctor or the emergency room of a hospital.

The vast number of sports injuries, though, are not serious. Sports physicians have worked out a four-part treatment that can be used with many of the minor sports injuries. They call this method RICE, using the first initials of the four steps.

Rest: The first rule when you are injured is to stop playing. Continuing to play with an injury may make you seem heroic. But it may also make the injury worse and lengthen your recovery time.

Ice: Chill the area of injury by applying ice right after the accident. This serves to close the blood vessels and controls any swelling or bleeding. The less fluid and blood in and around the injury, the faster the healing.

Compression: Pressing on the injured area, which is easily done with a tight elastic bandage, also helps to cut down the swelling.

Elevation: Raising the injured part uses gravity to drain away the fluids that the body sends to the site of an injury. It also promotes faster recovery.

Most muscle and tendon injuries can be treated with RICE. Once the pain, soreness and swelling are gone, you should start exercising to strengthen and build up the flexibility in the muscles. You should also be sure to follow the suggestions for good physical fitness and for warming up before sports participation.

Sports scientists are now learning about the importance of mental attitude after an injury. Athletes who think positively want very much to get better quickly. They are also willing to work hard to reach that goal. As a result, these positive thinkers seem to heal faster and recover function sooner than those who feel defeated and don't work as hard.

Whether you are striving to achieve better physical fitness and muscle tone, or just trying to avoid injuries and enjoy sports more, you have much to learn from the findings of modern sports medicine.

Sports medicine today is still a young science. Although it has already made many wonderful discoveries, all sorts of remarkable breakthroughs still lie ahead.

Growing, too, is the number of career opportunities in sports medicine. Many young people are planning to become physicians or psychologists specializing in sports medicine. Others are thinking about doing research on various aspects of the subject. Large numbers are studying to become trainers, therapists or exercise physiologists.

Sports medicine is an exciting and challenging field, with many opportunities for both men and women to make important contributions to the health and well-being of our nation.

We all gain from sports medicine! (UPI)

For Further Reading

Butt, Dorcas Susan. *Psychology of Sport.* New York: Van Nostrand, 1976.

Cavanagh, Peter R. *The Running Shoe Book.* Mountain View, CA: Anderson World, 1980.

Haycock, Christine. *Sports Medicine for the Athletic Female.* Arvnel, N.J.: Medical Economics, 1980.

Mirkin, Gabe and Marshall Hoffman. *The Sportsmedicine Book.* Boston: Little, Brown, 1978.

Singer, Robert N. *Myths and Truths in Sports Psychology.* New York: Harper & Row, 1975.

Strauss, Richard H. *Sports Medicine and Physiology.* Philadelphia: Saunders, 1972.

Suinn, Richard M. *Psychology in Sports.* Minneapolis: Burgess, 1980.

For Further Information

American Academy of Podiatric Sports Medicine
609 Park Forest Shopping Center
Dallas, TX 75234

American Alliance for Health, Physical Education, Recreation and
    Dance
1900 Association Drive
Reston, VA 22091

American College of Sports Medicine
1440 Monroe Street
Madison, WI 53706

American Orthopaedic Society for Sports Medicine
70 West Hubbard
Chicago, IL 60611

Index

121

INDEX